AF348982

Copyright: Lori Roberts 2019
All Rights Reserved

Release Date: 2019

ISBN: 978-1-943201-26-6
Library of Congress Control Number: 2019933962

All rights reserved. No part of this book may be reproduced or transmitted in any form or by any means, electronic or mechanical, including photocopying, recording, or by any information storage and retrieval system, without permission in writing from the publisher.

First Published by AM Ink Publishing LLC
www.AMInkPublishing.com

Lay Your Head on the Pillow

A bedtime story

Written by Lori Roberts

Illustrated by George Franco

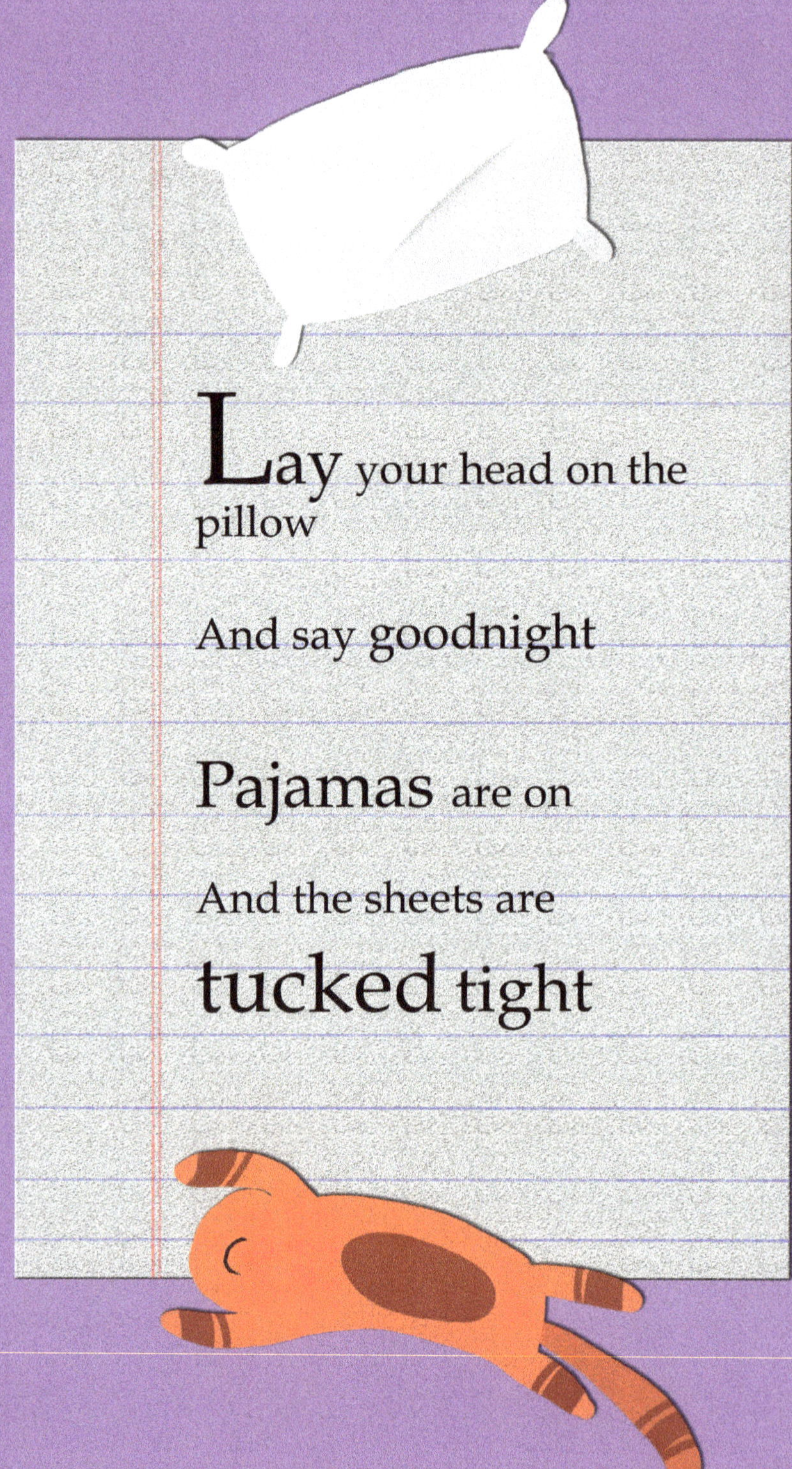

Lay your head on the pillow

And say goodnight

Pajamas are on

And the sheets are

tucked tight

The busy day has had its way

The beaming sun has lost its ray

The chirping
birds have said

goodbye

The silvery moon
is high in the

sky

Out of the tub so fresh and warm

Sweet
smells of

supper
are now

gone

No more
children
are at play

Time to settle
in and pray

The cozy house
is nice and
calm

Ready for a
brand new

day to dawn

Hoot
Hoot
Hoot
Hoot

The bright stars are all a twinkling

The wise old owls are all a singing

Hoot, *hoot*

Hoot, hoot...

P ajamas are on

The sheets are tucked

tight

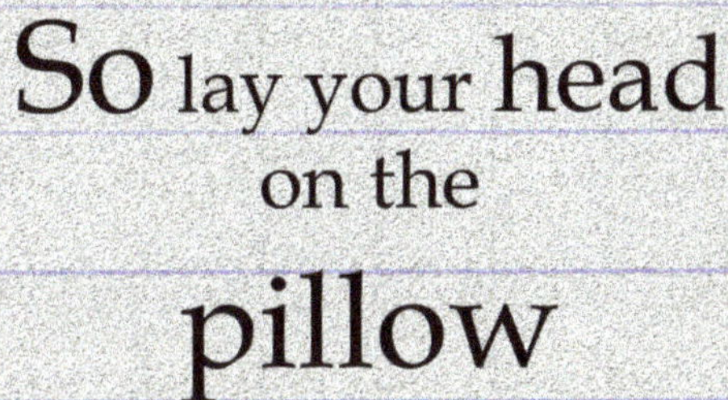

So lay your head
on the
pillow

And say

goodnight!

ABOUT THE AUTHOR

Lori Roberts was encouraged and inspired to write children's books while spontaneously telling stories to her young son at bedtime. With her tremendous love for children, Lori is passionate in her pursuit of bringing joy and positivity into the lives and homes of her readers. Lori is a native of California and mom of three beautiful children.

lorithewriter.com

ABOUT THE ILLUSTRATOR

George Franco is a prolific self-taught artist. As a student he would usually sit in the back of class and draw all day. He believes that anyone can reach their dreams with positivity, goal setting, and hard work. He has strong faith in the Lord and loves his family, his pets, nature, coffee, and good conversations. It is his dream to one day inspire and motivate the younger generation to find their paths in life.

georgefrancoart.weebly.com

www.ingramcontent.com/pod-product-compliance
Lightning Source LLC
LaVergne TN
LVHW052146130726
843272LV00009B/79